Charles Sumner

Explanation in reply to an assault

A speech prepared for the United States Senate, March, 1871

Charles Sumner

Explanation in reply to an assault
A speech prepared for the United States Senate, March, 1871

ISBN/EAN: 9783337150204

Printed in Europe, USA, Canada, Australia, Japan

Cover: Foto ©ninafisch / pixelio.de

More available books at **www.hansebooks.com**

"He, being Dead, yet Speaketh."

CHARLES SUMNER'S

EXPLANATION IN REPLY TO AN ASSAULT.

A SPEECH PREPARED FOR THE UNITED STATES SENATE,

MARCH, 1871.

"Poor me he fights, if that be fighting, where
He only cudgels and I only bear.
He stands and bids me stand : I must abide ;
For he 's the stronger, and is drunk beside."
JUVENAL, Sat. III. v. 273 - 277, Dryden's Version.

BOSTON:
LEE AND SHEPARD, PUBLISHERS.
NEW YORK:
CHARLES T. DILLINGHAM.
1878.

PERSONAL RELATIONS WITH THE PRESIDENT AND SECRETARY OF STATE.

Si rixa est, ubi tu pulsas, ego vapulo tantum.
Stat contra, starique jubet ; parere necesse. est.
Nam quid agas, cum te furiosus cogat, et idem
Fortior ?

JUVENAL, Sat. III. v. 273 – 277.

TO THE READER.

THIS statement was prepared in March shortly after the debate in the Senate ; but was withheld at that time from unwillingness to take part in the controversy, while able friends regarded the question of principle involved as above every personal issue. Yielding at last to various pressure, Mr. SUMNER concluded to present it at the recent called session of the Senate, but the Treaty with Great Britain and the case of the newspaper correspondents were so engrossing as to leave no time for anything else.

WASHINGTON, June, 1871.

INTRODUCTORY.

IN June, I think, 1871, I received from Mr. Sumner this "Explanation," with the following prefix, "Unpublished, — private and confidential, — not to go out of Mr. Bird's hands." I frequently urged him afterwards to make it public. His reply was, in substance, that he should not do it for personal vindication merely; that, so far as Mr. Motley was concerned, he thought the matter stood well enough before the public: but if the time should come when the ends of justice required its publication, he should remove the injunction of secrecy. While he lived I respected his injunction. After his death I felt that justice to his memory not only justified, but required me to make the "Explanation" public; just as his literary executors would regard it as not only proper, but it might, in their discretion, become a duty, to include this, with other "private and confidential" papers, with his works or in his biography. Accordingly, after conferring with Mr. Whitelaw Reid of the New York Tribune, I sent it to him, and it was published in that journal of April 6, 1874.

The publication attracted a good deal of attention, in a spirit very much depending upon the relations, per-

sonal and political, during his life, between the critics
and Mr. Sumner on the one hand and the persons
involved in the "Explanation" on the other. From one
of these classes I expected neither generosity nor justice. Not such defenders does the memory of CHARLES
SUMNER need; for, if invoked, they would only, as recent events have too clearly and sadly shown, have
done him injustice.

Mr. Sumner prefixed to the "Explanation" a passage
from Juvenal, of which I give Dryden's translation : —

> "Poor me he fights, if that be fighting, where
> He only cudgels and I only bear.
> He stands and bids me stand : I must abide ;
> For he 's the stronger, and is drunk beside."

An extraordinary spectacle has lately been presented
to the world. An ex-President of the United States,
travelling through Europe, has publicly proclaimed
CHARLES SUMNER as notoriously derelict in public duties, and a liar. The chief of his Cabinet has echoed
the same slanders. The transactions detailed in the
"Explanation" form the subject of a portion of these
charges. I do not enter upon a general examination
of these assaults, which, from their obvious malice and
improbability, were at once and instinctively repelled by
the whole truth-loving community. Full justice to Mr.
Sumner's memory has been done by the public press,
and specially by one of his most trusted friends, and
the public verdict against his defamers is substantially
unanimous. My only purpose in the present publica-

tion of the "Explanation" is to place in more permanent form his own reply to one of these assaults. The completeness of the vindication increases our regret that he does not live to reply to the other assaults lately made under responsible names, and also increases our amazement at the cowardice as well as the baseness of these slanders on the dead.

F. W. BIRD.

East Walpole, December 18, 1877.

AN EXPLANATION IN REPLY TO AN ASSAULT.

MR. SUMNER. While I was under trial before the Senate, on articles of impeachment presented by the Senator from Wisconsin [Mr. HOWE], I forbore taking any part in the debate, even in reply to allegations, asserted to be of decisive importance, touching my relations with the President and Secretary of State. All this was trivial enough; but numerous appeals to me from opposite parts of the country show that good people have been diverted by these allegations from the question of principle involved. Without intending in any way to revive the heats of that debate, I am induced to make a plain statement of facts, so that the precise character of those relations shall be known. I do this with unspeakable reluctance, but in the discharge of a public duty where the claims of patriotism are above even those of self-defence. The Senate and the country have an interest in knowing the truth of this matter, and so also has the Republican party, which cannot be indifferent to pretensions in its name; nor will anything but the completest frankness be proper for the occasion.

In overcoming this reluctance I am aided by Senators, who are determined to make me speak. The Senator from Wisconsin [Mr. HOWE], who appears as prosecuting officer, after alleging these personal relations

as the *gravamen* of accusation against me, — making
the issue pointedly on this floor and actually challeng-
ing reply, — not content with the opportunity of this
Chamber, hurried to the public press, where he repeated
the accusation, and now circulates it, as I am told, under
his frank, crediting it in formal terms to the liberal
paper in which it appeared, but without allusion to the
editorial refutation which accompanied it.   On still another occasion, appearing still as prosecuting officer, the
same Senator volunteered out of his own invention
to denounce me as leaving the Republican party, and
this he did, with infinite personality of language and
manner, in the very face of my speech to which he was
replying, where, in positive words, I declare that I
speak "for the sake of the Republican party," which I
hope to save from responsibility for wrongful acts, and
then, in other words making the whole assumption of
the Senator an impossibility, I announce, that in speaking for the Republican party it is "because from the
beginning I have been the faithful servant of that party
and aspire to see it strong and triumphant."   In the
face of this declared aspiration, in harmony with my
whole life, the Senator delivered his attack, and, assuming to be nothing less than Pope, launched against me
his bull of excommunication.   Then, again playing Pope,
he took back his thunder, with the apology that others
thought so, and this alleged understanding of others he
did not hesitate to set above my positive and contem-
poraneous language that I aspired to see the Republican
party strong and triumphant.   Then came the Senator
from Ohio [Mr. SHERMAN], who, taking up his vacation
pen, added to the articles of impeachment, by a supple-
mentary allegation, adopted by the Senator under a

misapprehension of facts. Here was another challenge. During all this time I have been silent. Senators have spoken and then rushed into print; but I have said nothing. They have had their own way with regard to me. It is they who leave me no alternative.

It is alleged that I have no personal relations with the President. Here the answer is easy. I have precisely the relations which he has chosen. On reaching Washington in December last, I was assured from various quarters, that the White House was angry with me, and soon afterward the public journals reported the President as saying to a Senator that if he were not President, he "would call me to account." What he meant I never understood, nor would I attribute to him more than he meant; but that he used the language reported I have no doubt, from information independent of the newspapers. I repeat that on this point I have no doubt. The same newspapers reported, also, that a member of the President's household, enjoying his peculiar confidence, taking great part in the St. Domingo scheme, had menaced me with personal violence. I could not believe the story except on positive, unequivocal testimony. That the menace was made on the condition of his not being an army officer I do not doubt. The member of the household, when interrogated by my excellent colleague [Mr. WILSON], positively denied the menace, but I am assured, on authority above question, that he has since acknowledged it, while the President still retains him in service, and sends him to this Chamber.

During this last session I have opposed the presidential policy on an important question ; but always

without one word touching motives, or one suggestion
of corruption on his part, although I never doubted that
there were actors in the business who could claim no
such immunity. It now appears that Fabens, who came
here as plenipotentiary to press the scheme, has conces-
sions to such amount that the diplomatist is lost in the
speculator. I always insisted that the President was
no party to any such transaction. I should do injustice
to my own feelings if I did not here declare my regret
that I could not agree with the President. I tried to
think as he did, but I could not. I listened to the
arguments on his side; but in vain. The adverse con-
siderations multiplied with time and reflection. To
those who know the motives of my life, it is superflu-
ous for me to add that I sought simply the good of my
country and Humanity, including especially the good
of the African race, to which our country owes so
much.

Already there was anger at the White House when
the scheme to buy and annex half an island in the
Caribbean Sea was pressed upon the Senate in legisla-
tive session, under the guise of appointing a Commission, and it became my duty to expose it. Here I was
constrained to show how, at very large expense, the
usurper Baez was maintained in power by the navy of
the United States, to enable him to sell his country,
while at the same time the independence of the Black
Republic was menaced, all of which was in violation
of International Law, and of the Constitution of the
United States, which reserves to Congress the power "to
declare war." What I said was in open debate, where the
record will speak for me. I hand it over to the most
careful scrutiny, knowing that the President can take

no just exception to it, unless he insists upon limiting proper debate, and boldly denies the right of a Senator to express himself freely on great acts of wrong. Nor will any Republican Senator admit that the President can impose his own sole will upon the Republican party. Our party is in itself a Republic with universal suffrage, and until a measure is adopted by the party no Republican President can make it a party test.

Much as I am pained in making this statement with regard to the President, infinitely more painful to me is what I must present with regard to the Secretary of State. Here again I remark that I am driven to this explanation. His strange and unnatural conduct toward me and his prompting of Senators, who, one after another, have set up my alleged relations with him as ground of complaint, make it necessary for me to proceed.

We were sworn as Senators on the same day, as far back as 1851, and from that distant time were friends, until the St. Domingo business intervened. Nothing could exceed our kindly relations in the past. On the evening of the inauguration of General Grant as President, he was at my house with Mr. Motley in friendly communion, and all uniting in aspirations for the new Administration. Little did Mr. Motley or myself imagine in that social hour that one of our little circle was so soon to turn upon us both.

Shortly afterward Mr. Fish became Secretary of State, and began his responsible duties by appealing to me for help. I need not say that I had pleasure in responding to his call, and that I did what I could most sincerely and conscientiously to aid him. Of much, from his

arrival down to his alienation on the St. Domingo business, I possess the written record. For some time he
showed a sympathy with the scheme almost as little as
my own. But as the President grew in earnestness the
Secretary yielded, until tardily he became its attorney.
Repeatedly he came to my house, pleading for the
scheme. Again and again he urged it; sometimes at
my house and sometimes at his own. I was astonished
that he could do so, and expressed my astonishment
with the frankness of old friendship. For apology he
announced that he was the President's friend, and took
office as such. "But," said I, "you should resign rather
than do this thing." This I could not refrain from
remarking on discovery from despatches in the State
Department, that the usurper Baez was maintained in
power by our navy. This plain act of wrong required
instant redress; but the Secretary astonished me again
by his insensibility to my appeal for justice. He maintained the President, as the President maintained Baez.
I confess that I was troubled.

At last, some time in June, 1870, a few weeks before
the St. Domingo treaty was finally rejected by the Senate, the Secretary came to my house about nine o'clock
in the evening, and remained till after the clock struck
midnight, the whole protracted visit being occupied in
earnest and reiterated appeal, that I should cease my
opposition to the Presidential scheme; and here he urged
that the election which made General Grant President
had been carried by him and not by the Republican
party, so that his desires were entitled to especial attention. In his pressure on me he complained that I had
opposed other projects of the President. In reply to my
inquiry he named the repeal of the Tenure-of-Office Act,

and the nomination of Mr. Jones as Minister to Brus-
sels, both of which the President had much at heart, and
he concluded with the St. Domingo treaty. I assured
the Secretary firmly and simply, that, seeing the latter
as I did with all its surroundings, my duty was plain,
and that I must continue to oppose it so long as it appeared to me wrong. He was not satisfied, and renewed
his pressure in various forms, returning to the point
again and again with persevering assiduity, that would
not be arrested, when at last, finding me inflexible, he
changed his appeal, saying, "Why not go to London?
I offer you the English mission. It is yours." Of his
authority from the President I know nothing. I speak
only of what he said. My astonishment was heightened
by indignation at this too palpable attempt to take me
from my post of duty; but I suppressed the feeling
which rose to the lips, and, reflecting that he was an old
friend and in my own house, answered gently, "We
have a Minister there who cannot be bettered." Thus
already did the mission to London begin to pivot on St.
Domingo.

I make this revelation only because it is important
to a correct understanding of the case, and because the
conversation from beginning to end was official in character, relating exclusively to public business, without
suggestion or allusion of a personal nature, and absolutely
without the slightest word on my part leading in the
most remote degree to any such overture, which was
unexpected as undesired. The offer of the Secretary
was in no respect a compliment or kindness, but in the
strict line of his endeavor to silence my opposition to
the St. Domingo scheme, as is too apparent from the
facts, while it was plain, positive, and unequivocal,

making its object and import beyond question. Had it been merely an inquiry, it were bad enough under the circumstances, but it was direct and complete as by a plenipotentiary.

Shortly afterward, being the day immediately following the rejection of the St. Domingo treaty, Mr. Motley was summarily removed, according to present pretence for an offending not only trivial and formal, but condoned by time, being a year old, — very much as Sir Walter Raleigh, after being released from the Tower to conduct a distant expedition as admiral of the fleet, was at his return beheaded on a judgment of fifteen years' standing. The Secretary in conversation and in correspondence with me undertook to explain the removal, insisting for a long time that he was "the friend of Mr. Motley"; but he always made the matter worse, while the heats of St. Domingo entered into the discussion.

At last, in January, 1871, a formal paper justifying the removal and signed by the Secretary was laid before the Senate. Glancing at this document I found, to my surprise, that its most salient characteristic was constant vindictiveness toward Mr. Motley, with effort to wound his feelings, and this was signed by one who had sat with him at my house in friendly communion and common aspiration on the evening of the inauguration of General Grant, and had so often insisted that he was "the friend of Mr. Motley"; while, as if it was not enough to insult one Massachusetts citizen in the public service, the same document, after a succession of flings and sneers, makes a kindred assault on me; and this is signed by one who so constantly called me "friend," and asked me for help. The Senator from Missouri [Mr. Schurz] has already directed attention to this assault, and has expressed his judgment upon it, — confessing that he "should not have failed to feel the insult," and then exclaiming with just indignation, "when such things are launched against any member of this body it becomes the American Senate to stand by him, and not to attempt to disgrace and degrade him because he shows the sensitiveness of a gentleman."* It is easy to see how this Senator regarded the conduct of the Secretary. Nor is its true character open to doubt, especially when we consider the context and how this full-blown personality naturally flowered out of the whole document.

Mr. Motley in his valedictory to the State Department had alluded to the rumor that he was removed on account of my opposition to the St. Domingo treaty. The document signed by the Secretary, while mingling most offensive terms with regard to his "friend" in London, thus turns upon his "friend" in Washington : —

"It remains only to notice Mr. Motley's adoption of a rumor, which had its origin in this city in a source bitterly, personally, and vindictively hostile to the President.

"Mr. Motley says it has been rumored that he was 'removed from the post of Minister to England' on account of the opposition made by an 'eminent Senator who honors me [him] with his friendship' to the San Domingo treaty.

"Men are apt to attribute the causes of their own failures or their own misfortunes to others than themselves, and to claim association or seek a partnership with real or imaginary greatness with which to divide their sorrows or their mistakes. There can be no question as to the identity of the eminent Senator at whose door Mr. Motley is willing to deposit the cause of his removal. But he is entirely mis-

* Congressional Globe, Debate of March 10, 1871.

taken in seeking a vicarious cause of his loss in confidence and favor, and it is unworthy of Mr. Motley's real merit and ability, and injustice to the venerable Senator alluded to (*to whose influence and urgency he was originally indebted for his nomination*) to attribute to him any share in the cause of his removal.

"Mr. Motley must know, or if he does not know it he stands alone in his ignorance of the fact, that many Senators opposed the San Domingo treaty *openly, generously, and with as much efficiency as did the distinguished Senator to whom he refers, and have nevertheless continued to enjoy the undiminished confidence and the friendship of the President,* than whom no man living is more tolerant of honest and manly differences of opinion, is more single or sincere in his desire for the public welfare, is more disinterested or regardless of what concerns himself, is more frank and confiding in his own dealings, *is more sensitive to a betrayal of confidence, or would look with more scorn and contempt upon one who uses the words and assurances of friendship to cover a secret and determined purpose of hostility.*" *

The eulogy of the President here is at least singular, when it is considered that every despatch of the Secretary of State is by order of the President; but it is evident that the writer of this despatch had made up his mind to set all rule at defiance. If beyond paying court to the President, even at the expense of making him praise himself, the concluding sentence of this elaborate passage, so full of gall from beginning to end, had any object, if it were anything but a mountain of words, it was an open attempt to make an official document the vehicle of personal insult to me, and this personal insult was signed " Hamilton Fish." As I became aware of it,

* Senate Executive Documents (No. 11, pp. 36, 37), 41st Cong. 3d Sess.

and found also that it was regarded by others in the same light, I was distressed and perplexed. I could not comprehend it. I knew not why the Secretary should step so far out of his way, in a manner absolutely without precedent, to treat me with ostentatious indignity, especially when I thought that for years I had been his friend, that I had never spoken of him except with kindness, and that constantly since assuming his present duties he had turned to me for help. This was more incomprehensible when I considered how utterly groundless were all his imputations. I have lived in vain if such an attempt on me can fail to rebound on its author.

Not lightly would I judge an ancient friend. For a time I said nothing to anybody of the outrage, hoping that perhaps the Secretary would open his eyes to the true character of the document he had signed and volunteer some friendly explanation. Meanwhile a proposition to resume negotiations was received from England, and the Secretary, it seems, desired to confer with me on the subject; but there was evident consciousness on his part that he had done wrong, for, instead of coming to me at once, he sent for Mr. Patterson of the Senate, and telling him that he wished to confer with me, added that he did not know precisely what were his relations with me and how I should receive him. Within a brief fortnight I had been in conference with him at the State Department and had dined at his house, besides about the same time making a call there. Yet he was in doubt about his relations with me. Plainly because since the conference, the dinner, and the call, the document signed by him had been communicated to the Senate, and the conscience-struck Secretary did not

know how I should take it. Mr. Patterson asked me
what he should report. I replied, that should the Secretary come to my house he would be received as an old
friend, and that at any time I should be at his service
for consultation on public business, but that I could not
conceal my deep sense of personal wrong received from
him absolutely without reason or excuse. That this
message was communicated by Mr. Patterson I cannot doubt, for the Secretary came to my house and there
was a free conference. How frankly I spoke on public
questions without one word on other things the Secretary knows. He will remember if any inquiry, remark,
or allusion escaped from me except in reference to public business. The interview was of business and nothing else.

On careful reflection it seemed to me plain, that,
while meeting the Secretary officially, it would not be
consistent with self-respect for me to continue personal
relations with one who had put his name to a document
which, after protracted fury toward another, contained a
studied insult to me, where the fury is intensified rather
than tempered by too obvious premeditation. Public
business must not suffer; but in such a case personal
relations naturally cease; and this rule I have followed
since. Is there any Senator who would have done less?
Are there not many who would have done more? I am
at a loss to understand how the Secretary could expect
anything beyond those official relations which I declared
my readiness at all times to maintain, and which, even
after his assault on me, he was willing to seek at my
own house. To expect more shows on his part grievous
insensibility to the thing he had done. Whatever one
signs he makes his own, and the Secretary, when he

signed this document, adopted a libel upon his friend,
and when he communicated it to the Senate he published the libel. Nothing like it can be shown in the
history of our Government. It stands alone. The Secretary is alone. Like Jean Paul in German literature
his just title will be "the only one." For years I have
known Secretaries of State, and often differed from
them, but never before did I receive from one anything
but kindness. Never before did a Secretary of State
sign a document libelling an associate in the public
service, and publish it to the world. Never before did a
Secretary of State so entirely set at defiance every sentiment of friendship. It is impossible to explain this
strange aberration except from the disturbing influence
of St. Domingo. But whatever its origin, its true character is beyond question.

As nothing like this State paper can be shown in the
history of our Government, so also nothing like it can
be shown in the history of other Governments. Not an
instance can be named in any country where a personage in corresponding official position has done such a
thing. The American Secretary is alone, not only in
his own country, but in all countries; "none but himself can be his parallel." Seneca in the Hercules Furens
has pictured him:

> "Quæris Alcidæ parem ?
> Nemo est nisi ipse."

He is originator and first inventor with all prerogatives
and responsibilities thereto belonging.

I have mentioned only one sally in this painful document; but the whole, besides its prevailing offensive-
ness, shows inconsistency with actual facts of my own
knowledge, which is in entire harmony with the reckless-

ness toward me and attests the same spirit throughout.
Thus we have the positive allegation that the death of
Lord Clarendon, June 27, 1870, "*determined the time
for inviting Mr. Motley to make place for a successor,*"
when, in point of fact, some time before his Lordship's
illness even, the Secretary had invited me to go to London as Mr. Motley's successor, — thus showing that the
explanation of Lord Clarendon's death was an afterthought when it became important to divert attention
from the obvious dependence of the removal upon the
defeat of the St. Domingo treaty.

A kindred inconsistency arrested the attention of the
"London Times" in its article of January 24, 1871, on
the document signed by the Secretary. Here, according
to this journal, the document supplied the means of
correction, since it set forth that on the 25th June,
two days before Lord Clarendon's death, Mr. Motley's
coming removal was announced in a London journal.
After stating the alleged dependence of the removal
upon the death of Lord Clarendon, the journal, holding
the scales, remarks, "And yet there is at least one cir-
cumstance appearing, *strange to say*, in Mr. Fish's own
despatch, which is *not quite consistent* with the explanation he sets up of Mr. Motley's recall." Then, after
quoting from the document, and mentioning that its own
correspondent at Philadelphia did on the 25th June
"send us a message that Mr. Motley was about to be
withdrawn," the journal mildly concludes, that, "as this
was two days before Lord Clarendon's death, which was
unforeseen here and could not have been expected in
the States, *it is difficult to connect the resolution to super-
sede the late American minister with the change at our
Foreign Office.*" The difficulty of the "Times" is increased
by the earlier incident with regard to myself.

Not content with making the removal depend upon the death of Lord Clarendon when it was heralded abroad, not only before the death of this minister had occurred but while it was yet unforeseen, the document seeks to antedate the defeat of the St. Domingo treaty, so as to interpose "weeks and months" between the latter event and the removal. The language is explicit. "The treaty," says the document, "*was admitted* to be practically dead, and was wanting only the formal action of the Senate *for weeks and months* before the decease of the illustrious statesman of Great Britain." Weeks and months! And yet during the last month, when the treaty "was admitted to be practically dead," the Secretary who signed the document passed three hours at my house, pleading with me to withdraw my opposition, and finally wound up by tender to me of the English mission, with no other apparent object than simply to get me out of the way.

Then again we have the positive allegation that the President embraced an. opportunity "to prevent any further misapprehension of his views through Mr. Motley by taking from him the right to discuss further the Alabama claims," whereas the Secretary in a letter to me at Boston, dated at Washington, October 9, 1869, informs me that the discussion of the question was withdrawn from London, "*because* [the italics are the Secretary's] we think that when renewed it can be carried on here with a better prospect of settlement than where the late attempt at a convention which resulted so disastrously and was conducted so strangely was had"; and what the Secretary thus wrote he repeated in conversation when we met, carefully making the transfer to Washington depend upon our advantage here, from the presence of the Senate, — thus showing that the pretext put forth to wound Mr. Motley was an afterthought.

Still further, the document signed by the Secretary alleges, by way of excuse for removing Mr. Motley, "the important public consideration of having a representative in sympathy with the President's views," whereas, when the Secretary tendered the mission to me, no allusion was made to "sympathy with the President's views," while Mr. Motley, it appears, was charged with agreeing too much with me, — all of which shows how little this matter had to do with the removal, and how much the St. Domingo business at the time was above any question of conformity on other things.

In the amiable passage already quoted there is a parenthesis which breathes the prevailing spirit. By way of aspersion on Mr. Motley and myself the country is informed that he was indebted for his nomination to "influence and urgency" on my part. Of the influence I know nothing; but I deny positively any "urgency." I spoke with the President on this subject once casually, on the stairs of the Executive Mansion, and then again in a formal interview. And here, since the effort of the Secretary, I shall frankly state what I said and how it was introduced. I began by remarking, that, with the permission of the President, I should venture to suggest the expediency of continuing Mr. Marsh in Italy, Mr. Morris at Constantinople, and Mr. Bancroft at Berlin, as all these exerted a peculiar influence and did honor to our country. To this list I proposed to add Dr. Howe in Greece, believing that he, too, would do honor to our country, and also Mr. Motley in London, who, I suggested, would have an influence there beyond his official

position. The President said that nobody should be
· sent to London who was not "right" on the claims
question, and he kindly explained to me what he meant
by "right." From this time I had no conversation with
him about Mr. Motley, until after the latter had left for
his post, when the President volunteered to express his
great satisfaction in the appointment. Such was the
extent of my "urgency"; nor was I much in advance of
the Secretary at that time, for he showed me what was
called the "brief" at the State Department for the
English mission with Mr. Motley's name at the head of
the list.

Other allusions to myself would be cheerfully for-
gotten if they were not made the pretext to assail Mr.
Motley, who is held to severe account for supposed dependence on me. If this were crime, not the Minister
but the Secretary should suffer, for it is the Secretary
and not the Minister who appealed to me constantly for
help, often desiring me to think for him, and more than
once to·hold the pen for him. But, forgetting his own
relations with me, the Secretary turns upon Mr. Motley,
who never asked me to think for him or to hold the
pen for him. Other things the Secretary also forgot.
He forgot that the blow he dealt, whether at Mr. Motley
or myself, rudely tore the veil from the past, so far as its
testimony might be needed in elucidation of the truth;
that the document he signed was a challenge and provo-
cation to meet him on the facts without reserve or
concealment; that the wantonness of assault on Mr.
Motley was so closely associated with that on me, that
any explanation I might make must be a defence of
him; that even if duty to the Senate and myself did
not require this explanation, there are other duties not

to be disregarded, among which is duty to the absent, who cannot be permitted to suffer unjustly, — duty to a much-injured citizen of Massachusetts, who may properly look to a Senator of his State for protection against official wrong, — duty also to a public servant insulted beyond precedent, who, besides writing and speaking most effectively for the Republican party and for this Administration, has added to the renown of our country by unsurpassed success in literature, commending him to the gratitude and good-will of all. These things the Secretary strangely forgot when he dealt the blow which tore the veil.

The crime of the Minister was dependence on me. So says the State paper. A simple narrative will show who is the criminal. My early relations with the Secretary have already appeared, and how he began by asking me for help, practising constantly on this appeal. A few details will be enough. At once, on his arrival to assume his new duties, he asked my counsel about appointing Mr. Bancroft Davis Assistant Secretary of State, and I advised the appointment, without sufficient knowledge I am inclined to believe now. Then followed the questions with Spain growing out of Cuba, which were the subject of constant conference, where he sought me repeatedly and kindly listened to my opinions. Then came the instructions for the English mission known as the despatch of May 16, 1869. At each stage of these instructions I was in the counsels of the Secretary. Following my suggestion he authorized me to invite Mr. Motley in his name to prepare the "memoir" or essay on our claims, which, notwithstanding its entirely confidential character, he drags before the world, for purpose of assault, in a manner clearly unjustifiable.

Then, as the despatch was preparing, he asked my help especially in that part relating to the concession of belligerent rights. I have here the first draft of this important passage in pencil and in my own handwriting, varying in no essential respect from that adopted. Here will be found the distinction on which I have always ⁻ insisted, that while other Powers conceded belligerent rights to our rebels, it was in England only that the concession was supplemented by acts causing direct damage to the United States. Not long afterward, in August, 1869, when the British storm had subsided, I advised that the discussion should be renewed by an elaborate communication, setting forth our case in length and breadth, but without any estimate of damages, throwing upon England the opportunity, if not the duty, of making some practical proposition. Adopting this recommendation, the Secretary invited me to write the despatch. I thought it better that it should be done by another, and I named for this purpose an accomplished gentleman, whom I knew to be familiar with the question, and he wrote the despatch. This paper, bearing date September 25, 1869, is unquestionably the ablest in the history of the present Administration, unless we except the last despatch of Mr. Motley.

In a letter dated at Washington, October 15, 1869, and addressed to me at Boston, the Secretary describes this paper in the following terms: " The despatch to Motley (which I learn by a telegram from him has been received) is a calm, *full* review of our entire case, making no demand, no valuation of damages, but I believe covering all the ground and all the points that have been made on our side. I hope that it will meet your views. I *think* it will. It leaves the question with Great Britain

to determine when any negotiations are to be renewed."
The Secretary was right in his description. It was
"a *full* review of our whole case," "covering all the
ground and all the points"; and it did meet.my views,
as the Secretary thought it would, especially where it
arraigned so strongly that fatal concession on belligerent
rights on the ocean, which in any faithful presentment
of the national cause will always be the first stage of
evidence, since without this precipitate and voluntary
act the common law of England was a positive protection against the equipment of a corsair ship, or even the
supply of a blockade-runner for unacknowledged rebels.
The conformity of this despatch with my views was rec-
ognized by others besides the Secretary. It is well known
that Lord Clarendon did not hesitate in familiar conversation to speak of it as " Mr. Sumner's speech over
again"; while another English personage said that it
out-Sumnered Sumner." And yet with his name signed
to this despatch, written at my suggestion, and in entire
conformity with my views, as admitted by him and rec-
ognized by the English Government, the Secretary taunts
Mr. Motley for supposed harmony with me on this very
question. This taunt is still more unnatural when it is
known that this despatch is in similar conformity with
the " memoir " of Mr. Motley, and was evidently written
with knowledge of that admirable document, where the
case of our country is stated with perfect mastery. But
the story does not end here.

On the communication of this despatch to the British
Government, Mr. Thornton was instructed to ascertain
what would be accepted by our Government, when the
Secretary, under date of Washington, November 6, 1869,
reported to me this application, and then, after express-

ing unwillingness to act on it until he "could have an opportunity of consulting" me, he wrote, "When will you be here? Will you either note what you think will be sufficient to meet the views of the Senate and of the country, or *will you formulate such proposition?*" After this responsible commission, the letter winds up with the earnest request: "Let me hear from you *as soon as you can* [the italics are the Secretary's], and I should like to confer with you at the earliest convenient time." On my arrival at Washington the Secretary came to my house at once, and we conferred freely. St. Domingo had not yet sent its shadow into his soul.

It is easily seen that here was constant and reiterated appeal to me, especially on our negotiations with England, and yet in the face of this testimony, where he is the unimpeachable witness, the Secretary is pleased to make Mr. Motley's supposed relations with me the occasion of insult to him, while, as if this were not enough, he crowns his work with personal assault on me, — all of which, whether as regards Mr. Motley or me, is beyond comprehension.

How little Mr. Motley merited anything but respect and courtesy from the Secretary is attested by all who know his eminent position in London, and the service he rendered to his country. Already the London press, usually slow to praise Americans when strenuous for their country, has furnished its voluntary testimony. The "Daily News" of August 16, 1870, spoke of the insulted minister in these terms: —

"We are violating no confidence in saying that all the hopes of Mr. Motley's official residence in England have been amply fulfilled, and that the announcement of his unexpected and unexplained recall was received with extreme astonishment and unfeigned regret. The vacancy he leaves cannot possibly be filled by a Minister more sensitive to the honor of his Government, more attentive to the interests of his country, and more capable of uniting the most rigorous performance of his public duties with the high-bred courtesy and conciliatory tact and temper that make those duties easy and successful. Mr. Motley's successor will find his mission wonderfully facilitated by the firmness and discretion that have presided over the conduct of American affairs in this country during too brief a term, too suddenly and unaccountably concluded."

The London press had not the key to this extraordinary transaction. It knew not the potency of the St. Domingo spell; nor its strange influence over the Secretary, even breeding insensibility to instinctive amenities, and awakening peculiar unfriendliness to Mr. Motley, so amply certified afterward in an official document under his own hand,—all of which burst forth with more than the tropical luxuriance of the much-coveted island.

I cannot disguise the sorrow with which I offer this explanation. In self-defence and for the sake of truth do I now speak. I have cultivated forbearance, and hoped from the bottom of my heart that I might do so to the end. But beyond the call of the public press has been the defiant challenge of Senators, and also the consideration sometimes presented by friends, that my silence might be misinterpreted. Tardily and most reluctantly I make this record, believing it more a duty to the Senate than to myself, but a plain duty to be performed in all simplicity without reserve. Having nothing to conceal, and willing always to be judged by the truth, I court the fullest inquiry, and shrink from no conclusion founded on an accurate knowledge of the case.

If this narration enables any one to see in clearer light the injustice done to Mr. Motley, then have I performed a further duty too long postponed; nor will it be doubted by any honest nature, that since the assault of the Secretary he was entitled to that vindication which is found in a statement of facts within my own knowledge. Anything short of this would be a license to the Secretary in his new style of State paper, which, for the sake of the public service and of good-will among men, must be required to stand alone, in the isolation which becomes its abnormal character. Plainly without precedent in the past, it must be without chance of repetition in the future.

Here I stop. My present duty is performed when I set forth the simple facts, exhibiting those personal relations which have been drawn in question, without touching the questions of principle behind.

THE COMPLETE WORKS

OF

CHARLES SUMNER.

PUBLISHERS' ADVERTISEMENT.

" Not ordinary addresses, — they remind us rather of the Orations of De-
mosthenes, — of times when men of note, endowed with the highest understand-
ing, gave full vent to the feelings that possessed them, and stirred their
country with a fervid eloquence which was all the more impressive because it
related to the political circumstances in which their country was placed." —
EDINBURGH JOURNAL.

THE COMPLETE WORKS

OF

CHARLES SUMNER

In Fourteen elegant Crown 8vo Volumes, with Portrait,
Notes, and Index.

"The twelfth volume of the sumptuous edition of Charles Sumner's works
which Lee and Shepard are publishing is now ready, and is being distributed to the
subscribers. It is a volume of more than common interest. It contains the monograph entitled 'Prophetic Voices concerning America,' hitherto published sepa-
rately; 'Are we a Nation,' the thoughtful and important address delivered at the
Cooper Institute in New York in 1868; a half-dozen speeches concerning the impeachment of Andrew Johnson, delivered in the Senate Chamber; an address on
'Financial Reconstruction through Public Faith and Specie Payments,'—a subject of quite as vital interest now as when delivered; and an address on the Issues
of the Presidential Election of 1868, which was delivered at City Hall, Cambridge,
in October of that year. There are a number of brief letters and speeches on various political subjects, which bring the volume up to nearly five hundred and fifty
pages. Two more volumes will complete the publication."—*Boston Journal.*

Price per volume, Fine English Cloth $3.00
"   "   Half Calf, Gilt Extra, Library Edition   5.00

Sold by Subscription.

PUBLISHED BY LEE AND SHEPARD,

Nos. 41 – 45 Franklin Street, Boston.

The Publishers invite attention to the following extracts taken from the mass of communications and testimonials received from prominent and leading men on both sides of the Atlantic : —

From Francis Lieber.

The complete works of Senator Sumner will have a high value for the earnest student who desires to trace the causes of some of the greatest movements in our times, — the times of political Reformation. They will have a great value in point of Political Ethics, of Statesmanship (or what the ancients called Politics), and in point of the Psychology of our own nation, in point of the Law of Nations and for every English scholar and admirer of eloquence. Not only will the works of Senator Sumner, after whose title, in Rome, the words " Four Times in Succession " would have been put, be gladly received by every reflecting public man in America, but also by every high-minded Nationalist and lover of freedom in Europe.

From William Cullen Bryant.

I am glad to learn that Mr. Sumner's works are to be collected and published under his own superintendence and revision. He ranks among our most eminent public men, and never treats of any subject without shedding new light upon it, and giving us reason to admire both his ability and the extent and accuracy of his information.

From Ralph Waldo Emerson.

I learn with interest that you are preparing to publish a complete collection of Mr. Sumner's writings and speeches. They will be the history of the Republic in the last twenty-five years, as told by a brave, perfectly honest, and well-instructed man, with large social culture, and relations to all eminent persons. Few public men have left records more important, — none more blameless. Mr. Sumner's large ability, his careful education, his industry, his early dedication to public affairs, his power of exhaustive statement, and his pure character, — qualities rarely combined in one man, — have been the strength and pride of the Republic. In Massachusetts, the patriotism of his constituents has treated him with exceptional regard. The ordinary complaisances expected of a candidate have not been required of him, it being known that his service was one of incessant labor, and that he had small leisure to plead his own cause, and less to nurse his private interests. There will be the more need of the careful publication in a permanent form of these vindications of political liberty and morality.

I hope that Mr. Sumner's contributions to some literary journals will not be omitted in your collection.

From John G. Whittier.

It gives me much satisfaction to learn that the entire speeches of Mr. Sumner are about to be published. Apart from their great merit in a literary and scholastic point of view, and as exhaustive arguments upon questions of the highest import, they have a certain historic value which will increase with the lapse of time. Whoever wishes to understand the legislation and political and moral progress of the country for the last quarter of a century, must study these remarkable speeches. I am heartily glad the publication has been determined upon, and wish it the success it deserves.

From Horace Greeley.

I hail it as a cheering sign of the times that the speeches and writings of Charles Sumner are to be published complete. We live in an age of inconsiderate gabble, when too many make speeches "on the spur of the moment," and "now that I am up," say whatever may chance to come into their heads. Mr. Sumner sufficiently respects his associates and his countrymen to speak with due preparation, and only when he feels that silence would be dereliction. "Not to stir without great arguments" is his rule; hence his speeches are not only a part of his country's history, but a very creditable and instructive part of it. In an age of venality and of reckless calumny, no man has ever doubted the purity of his motives, the singleness of his aims; and if the august title of statesman has been deserved by any American of his age, he is that American. I trust his collected writings will receive wide currency, as I am sure they will command universal consideration.

From Samuel G. Howe.

I think that your proposed edition of Mr. Sumner's Speeches will do much good. His public career teaches a lesson which should be learned by all who aspire to usefulness and true greatness. The source of his popularity and influence, creditable alike to him and to the people, is an intuitive perception of the right and firm faith in its prevalence. To him, whatever is right is ever expedient. Be the political horizon ever so dark, he knows the direction of the pole-star, and steers boldly towards it. In opposing storms, while ordinary politicians, like sailing ships, tack and keep as near the wind as seems safe, he, like the steamer, steers straight in the wind's eye; and though he may, for the moment, make no headway, he swerves not, larboard nor starboard. Most statesmen and politicians represent certain doctrines or party interests; while he represents the moral sense of the people. Where that sense is most developed, there he is best understood and most esteemed. A new edition of his Speeches will help to develop it still more; and it is for that end, rather than building a monument to him, that his friends ought to co-operate for your success.

From Caleb Cushing.

I think the speeches, discourses, and miscellaneous papers of Mr. Sumner eminently deserve to be collected and published in a complete form. Whatever difference of opinion there may be in the country concerning the various political doctrines which in his long Senatorial career he has so earnestly and so steadily maintained, certain it is that his productions constitute an essential part of our public history as well in foreign as in domestic relations; and they are characterized by such qualities of superior intellectual power, cultivated eloquence, and great and general accomplishment and statesmanship, as entitle them to a high and permanent place in the political literature of the United States.

From James Russell Lowell.

I am glad to hear that you have undertaken an edition of Mr. Sumner's collected works. There is a manifest propriety in this, for not only has he made many contributions to literature proper, but his speeches have been elaborated with so much care, and illustrated from so wide a field of reading, that letters claim in them an equal share with politics. Whatever view may be taken of them, they form an essential part of our history for the last twenty years.

Though I have sometimes been unable to go along with Mr. Sumner in his application of opinions, with which I mainly agreed, to questions of immediate policy, I have always duly honored the sincerity of his convictions, and his courage in maintaining them. A life of high aims, public purposes, and sustained integrity, has been fully rewarded by a constituency of which that which he represents in the Senate forms but a small portion, and I cannot doubt that your enterprise will be welcomed as it deserves by all who know how to appreciate an eloquence which has so largely confined itself to the discussion of principles, and a culture which is an ornament to the Senate.

From George William Curtis.

I am very glad to learn that the complete works of Charles Sumner will soon be published.

Mr. Sumner's public life has been illustrious for his unswerving devotion to human liberty, and his service in the great struggle of the last twenty years will be always gratefully remembered. Even the qualities that now alienate a certain sympathy will then be seen to have been necessary to his work.

His speeches are an essential part of the history of those times, and are distinguished by their ample knowledge and their lofty tone. There is no American citizen who may not study his works with instruction, no American statesman who may not contemplate his career with advantage.

From Benjamin F. Butler.

I am much pleased to learn that a complete compilation of Mr. Sumner's speeches and letters is to be published.

They are a desideratum for the times. The history of the anti-slavery contest in Congress is therein written in living language, because each speech made of itself an epoch in the struggle. The almost providential accident of one vote gave to Mr. Sumner the position ot leader in the great work which has purged the institutions, the very constitution of the country, from the sin and wrong of slavery; and nobly has he filled it; better, indeed, than could have been done by any other man in the nation. The virulent opposition which he met in the great task which he undertook required his varied accomplishments and learning, his untiring industry, and unswerving devotion to principle, — qualities seldom united in one. The history of the regeneration of Republican Democracy in the western world would not be complete without the volumes you are about to publish.

From Henry Wilson.

I am really gratified to learn that you are to publish the complete works of Mr. Sumner, under his own supervision. During the past twenty-five years I have known him, watched his course as a public man, heard and read his speeches, and know how he has consecrated talents and learning to the rights of man and the enduring interests of his country. His speeches have largely contributed to produce the grand results that cheer and bless us, and I am sure they will be read with increasing interest, not only for the topics discussed, but for their learning and eloquence.

From Wendell Phillips.

I am glad you are to give us a complete collection of Mr. Sumner's Speeches. His part and place have been such in the last twenty years, that his career is largely the history of the Nation. His speeches cover the most important and interesting questions we have been called to meet. Years ago the easy sneer was that he was a man of "one idea," — dealt only with one question, or one class of questions.

But Mr. Sumner has been one of the most industrious, perhaps the most industrious, Senator that Massachusetts has ever given to the national councils. His mind has been more comprehensive than that of any of his predecessors. He has grappled with all the great problems of the day ; and so thoroughly, so exhaustively, as to leave nothing to desire.

Accurate, profoundly learned, always in the van, fearless, wielding a most commanding influence, his speeches will be the most valuable contribution possible to the literature of politics and reform. They have " made history," and will naturally be the best reliance of those who shall study our times, as his career will be, both for students and statesmen, one of the noblest examples.

By Hon. John P. Hale, in the United States Senate, August 27, 1851, in the debate after Mr. Sumner's Speech entitled " Freedom National, Slavery Sectional."

I feel bound to say that the Honorable Senator from Massachusetts has, so far as his own personal fame and reputation are concerned, done enough, by the effort he has made here to-day to place himself side by side with the first orators of antiquity, and as far ahead of any living American orator as freedom is ahead of slavery. I believe he has founded a new era to-day in the history of the politics and of the eloquence of the country; and that, in future generations, the young men of this nation will be stimulated to effort by the record of what an American Senator has this day done, to which all the appeals drawn from ancient history would be entirely inadequate. Yes, sir, he has to-day made a draft upon the gratitude of the friends of humanity and of liberty that will not be paid through many generations, and the memory of which shall endure as long as the English language is spoken, or the history of this Republic forms part of the annals of the world. That, sir, is what I feel, and if I had one other feeling, or could indulge in it in reference to that effort, it would be a feeling alway, that it was not in me to tread, even at a humble distance, in the path he has so nobly and eloquently illustrated.

From Hannibal Hamlin.

I learn with great pleasure that the complete works of Hon. Charles Sumner are being now prepared, and will soon be published.

The high position which Mr. Sumner has so long and so honorably maintained as one of the leading minds of the nation, his intimate connection with and lead in the great measure of the abolition of slavery, and all the great questions of the late war, and those involved in a just settlement of the same, render it a desideratum that his works should be published.

From S. Austin Allibone.

I have been in the habit for some years past, from time to time, of urging my valued friend, Mr. Sumner, to publish a collective edition of his speeches. You may therefore imagine the pleasure with which I have received the announcement that you are now engaged in the publication of a uniform edition of his complete works.

One of the favorite pupils of Judge Story, who considered him rather as a son than as his pupil (see Story's Life and Letters, Vol. II. p. 39), the endeared friend of Prescott, Wheaton, the Earl of Carlisle, and many of the most distinguished scholars on both sides of the Atlantic, Mr. Sumner's opportunities of instruction by contact with great minds have matured the scholarship of which the broad and deep foundations were laid in the laborious days and nights of collegiate and private application.

The " fulness " of his mind and the ease with which he draws from the vast stores of memory " things new and old " to illustrate the truths which he enforces, the errors he exposes, or the themes he propounds, are indeed marvellous! See for instance, his oration, entitled, " The Scholar, the Jurist, the Artist, the Philanthropist," (1846), of which Prescott wrote: " I have read or rather listened to it, notes and all, with the greatest interest; and when I say that my expectations have not been disappointed after having heard it cracked up so, I think you will think it praise enough. The most happy conception has been carried out admirably, as if it were the most natural order of things, without the least constraint or violence." (Ticknor's Life of Prescott, p. 378.) Among his late speeches, take his graphic and glowing portraiture of Alaska, over the sterile soil of which the light of his genius has cast a glow of bloom and beauty; which as a geographical and topographical monograph might have excited the envy of D'Anville or Humboldt. A complete collection of his works, fully rounded by a copious analytical index of subjects discussed, topics referred to, and facts adduced, would be an invaluable treasury to the scholar, the historian, and the general reader.

From Edwin P. Whipple.

I am glad to hear that a complete edition of Senator Sumner's works is to be published.

Not to speak of the eminent literary merit of his speeches and addresses, they are specially valuable as having contributed in an important degree to " make history " during the past twenty-five years. Many of his senatorial efforts are not so much speeches as events. They have palpably advanced the cause of honesty, justice, freedom, and humanity. It is to the immense honor of Massachusetts that she has had for so long a time so noble a representative in Washington of her sentiments and ideas, — one whose abundant learning, richness and reach of thought, and statesman-like forethought are combined with a philanthropy so frank and a spirit so intrepid.

A complete edition of the works of a statesman so variously endowed, and who has treated so many subjects with such a masterly command of knowledge, reasoning, and eloquence, cannot fail to be widely circulated.

From Hunt's Merchants' Magazine.

The Orations of Mr. Sumner belong to the literature of America. They are as far superior to the endless number of orations and speeches which are delivered throughout the country as the works of a polished, talented, and accomplished author surpass the ephemeral productions of a day. Pure and highly classical in style, strong in argument, and rich and glowing in imagery, and in some parts almost reaching the poetic, they come to the reader always fresh, always interesting and attractive. In one respect these orations surpass almost all others. It is in the elevation of sentiment, the high and lofty moral tone and grandeur of thought which they possess. In this particular, united with their literary merit, these productions have no equal among us. The one on the "True Grandeur of Nations" stands forth by itself, like a serene and majestic image, cut from the purest Parian marble. Those on "Peace and War," and two or three others, possess equal merit, equal beauty, and equal purity and dignity of thought. In our view, these orations approach nearer the models of antiquity than those of any other writer amongst us, unless it be Webster, whom Sumner greatly surpasses in moral tone and dignity of thought.

Many of the distinguished statesmen and scholars of our country, now deceased, left on record their opinion of the character and value of Mr. Sumner's public services. From among these a few are selected.

From John Quincy Adams.

In a letter addressed to Mr. Sumner immediately after the delivery of the celebrated oration, "The Scholar, the Artist, the Jurist, the Philanthropist," Mr. Adams remarks: —

"It is a gratification to me to have the opportunity to repeat the thanks which I so cordially gave you at the close of your oration last Thursday, and of which the sentiment offered by me at the dinner-table,* was but an additional pulsation from the same head. I trust I may now congratulate you on the felicity, first of your selection of your subject, and secondly, by its consummation in the delivery. But you will indulge me in the frankness and candor, which if they had not been the laws of a long life, would yet be imperative duties on its last stage, in the remark that the pleasure with which I listened to your discourse was inspired far less by the success, and all but universal acceptance and applause of the present moment, than by the vista of the future which it opened to my view. Casting my eyes back no further than the Fourth of July of the last year, when you set all the vipers of Alecto hissing, by proclaiming the Christian law of Universal Peace and Love, and then casting them forward perhaps, not much

------

* The sentiment was, — "The memory of the Scholar, the Jurist, the Artist, and the Philanthropist, and — not the memory, but the long life of the kindred spirit who has this day embalmed them all."

further, but beyond my own allotted time, I see you have a mission to perform. I look from Pisgah to the Promised Land, — you must enter upon it."

From Edward Everett.

The late Hon. Edward Everett, in acknowledging the receipt of the two-volume edition of Mr. Sumner's speeches, published several years ago, said : —

" Their contents, most of which were well known to me already, are among the most finished productions of their class in our language, — in any language. I am sure they will be read and admired, as long as anything English or American is remembered."

From Chancellor Kent, of New York.

Of Mr. Sumner's speech on " The Right of Search on the Coast of Africa," Chancellor Kent remarked in a private letter : —

" I have no hesitation in subscribing to it as entirely sound, logical, and conclusive. There is no doubt of it, and the neatness and elegance with which it is written are delightful."

The same eminent authority remarks of Mr. Sumner's Oration on " The True Grandeur of Nations," —

" I think the doctrine is well sustained by principle, and the precepts of the Gospel. The historical and classical illustrations are beautiful and apposite, and I cannot but think that such cogent and eloquent appeals to the heads and consciences of our people, must have effect."

Of Mr. Sumner's sketch of Hon. John Pickering, Chancellor Kent wrote : —

" The biographical sketch of that extraordinary scholar and man, John Pickering, is admirable, and most beautifully and eloquently drawn."

Of Mr. Sumner's celebrated " Phi Beta Kappa Address," he remarks : " I think it to be one of the most splendid productions, in point of diction and eloquence, that I have ever read."

From Martin Van Buren.

President Van Buren said of the oration on the "Law of Human Progress": —

"It has, bo assured, afforded me the highest satisfaction to find a production affording such incontestable proof of the learning and great intellect of its author, — proceeding from a gentleman who has established the strongest claims to my admiration and respect."

From Judge Story.

Of Mr. Sumner's oration on "The True Grandeur of Nations," Judge Story remarked in a private letter: —

"It is certainly a very striking production, and will fully sustain Mr. Sumner's reputation for high talent, various reading, and exact scholarship. There are a great many passages in it which are wrought out with an exquisite finish, and elegance of diction, and classical style . . . . . In many parts of the discourse I have been struck with the strong resemblance which it bears to the manly, moral enthusiasm of Sir James Mackintosh."

From William Jay.

I have just received your very acceptable present, — acceptable from my esteem for the writer and for the great truths contained in the volumes, expressed with the elegance of the scholar and the fearless integrity of the Christian. When called to account for the use you have made of the talents intrusted to you, these volumes will testify that you have labored to do good in your day and generation.

In this connection the estimate entertained of Mr. Sumner by leading men in England, will be of interest. From the great multitude of similar opinions, the following are selected: —

From the Edinburgh Journal.

Mr. Sumner's lectures are not ordinary addresses, — they remind us rather of the orations of Demosthenes, of times when men of note, endowed with the highest understanding, gave full vent to the feelings that possessed them, and stirred their country with a fervid eloquence which was all the more impressive because it related to the political circumstances in which their country was placed.

We have in our possession many of Mr. Sumner's speeches, and we confess that, for depth and accuracy of thought, for fulness of historical information, and for a species of gigantic morality which treads all sophistry under foot, and rushes at once to the right conclusion, we know not a single orator, speaking the English tongue, who ranks as his superior. He combines, to a remarkable extent, the peculiar features of our British Emancipationists, the perseverance of Granville Sharpe, the knowledge of Brougham, the enthusiasm of Wilberforce, and a courage, which, as he is still a young man, may be expected to tell powerfully on the destinies of the Republic.

From Richard Cobden.

You have made the most noble contribution of any modern writer, to the cause of Peace.

From the London Examiner.

We would recommend a close and earnest study of the speech on the Fugitive Slave Act, made by Mr. Charles Sumner in the Senate of the United States on the 26th of last August (1852). That speech will reward perusal. Apart from its noble and effective eloquence, it is one of the closest and most convincing arguments we have ever read on the policy of the earlier and greater, as contrasted with that of the later and meaner, statesmen of America.

From a Letter of Lord Shaftesbury to the London Times.

Let us take a few lines descriptive of the terrible enactment from the speech of the Hon. Charles Sumner, one of those powerful intellects and noble hearts that have shone so brightly in our sister country, in the Senate of the United States. . . . . What noble eloquence! Carry these words, sir, by the vehicle of your almost universal paper to the press of every country, and to the heart of every human being — man, woman, or child — who has ever heard the divine rule, "Whatsoever ye would that men should do unto you, do ye even so to them."

From the Poet, Samuel Rogers.

In a letter to the author, the poet, Samuel Rogers, wrote: " What can I say to you in return for your admirable oration ? (' The True Grandeur of Nations.') I can only say with what pleasure I have read it, and how truly every pulse of my heart beats in accordance with yours on the subject. . . . . Again and again must I thank you."

From Lord Carlisle.

Lord Carlisle in his preface to an English edition of " Uncle Tom's Cabin," in some pleasant reminiscences of interviews with " my own most valued friend, Mr. Charles Sumner," remarks : —

" And now while I have been writing these lines, I have received the speech he has lately delivered in Congress on the bearings of the Fugitive Slave Law, which by the closeness of its logic, and the masculine vigor of its eloquence, proves to me how all the perfections of his mind have grown up to, and been dilated with the inspiration of the cause which he has now made his own.

From Chambers's Edinburgh Journal.

The oration (" The True Grandeur of Nations ") of Mr. Sumner, for taste, eloquence, and scholarship, as well as for fearless intrepidity, has been rarely equalled in modern harangues.

From the London Quarterly Review.

He presents in his own person a decisive proof that an American gentleman, without official rank or wide-spread reputation, by dint of courtesy, candor, an entire absence of pretension, an appreciative spirit, and a cultivated mind, may be received on a perfect footing of equality in the best circles, social, political, and intellectual, which, be it observed, are hopelessly inaccessible to the itinerant note-taker who never gets beyond the outskirts of the show-houses.